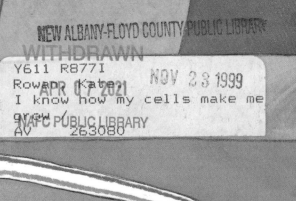

For Katie and Hannah
K. McE.

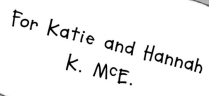

CONSULTANTS: Dr. Rupert Negus and Dr. Helena Scott,
and with thanks to Viv French

First U.S. edition 1999

Library of Congress Cataloging-in-Publication Data is available.

Library of Congress Catalog Card Number 98-45215

ISBN 0-7636-0502-6

2 4 6 8 10 9 7 5 3 1

This book was typeset in Soupbone.
The illustrations were done in colored pencil and watercolors.

Printed in Hong Kong

Candlewick Press
2067 Massachusetts Avenue
Cambridge, Massachusetts 02140

I Know How My Cells Make Me Grow

KATE ROWAN

illustrated by
KATHARINE McEWEN

CANDLEWICK PRESS
CAMBRIDGE, MASSACHUSETTS

"Help!" squeaked Sam.

"I'm stuck! My sweater shrank!"

"Oh, no it didn't," said Mom.
"You just got bigger.
Let's get that sweater off
and take a look at
your height chart."

Sam stood against the chart.

"Wow!" he said.

"I'm halfway up the dinosaur's neck!"

"Goodness!" said Mom. "You've grown
2 whole inches since I last measured you."

"I know why I'm growing so fast," said Sam.
"It's all the exercises
we've been doing in
gym class."

Mom smiled. "They may have helped a little,
but mainly it's because parts of your
body are getting bigger. Your **bones**
and your **muscles** and your **skin**
are growing—and you are, too."

"I know about **bones** and **muscles** and **skin**," said Sam.

"**Bones** hold me up. If I didn't have any, I'd be all floppy, like a tent with no poles.

And **muscles** let me move around. And my **skin** protects my insides from germs and stuff."

"That's right," said Mom.
"Come on—let's
clean up this room
before breakfast."

"Okay," said Sam.
"But how do **bones** and
muscles and **skin** grow?
Do they stretch like
rubber bands?"

"Not exactly," Mom said.
"Most of your body is made
of tiny things called **cells**.
When you grow, it's because
your **bone cells** are making
more **bone cells**, and your
muscle cells are making
more **muscle cells**, and..."

"I know! I know!"
shouted Sam.
"My **skin cells** are
making more **skin cells**!"

13

"Exactly," said Mom.

"You have lots of different kinds of **cells** in your body—about 200 I think—and each kind is a different shape.

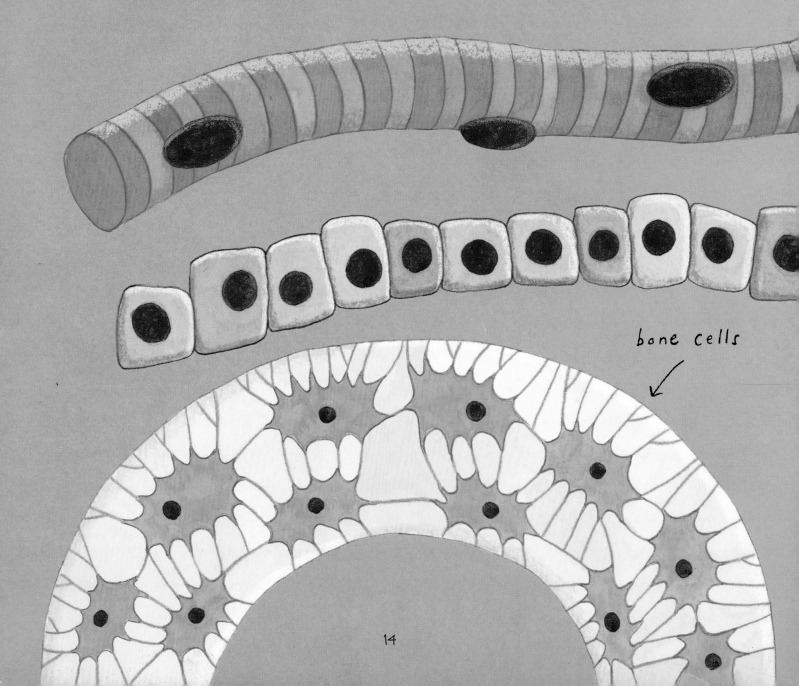

bone cells

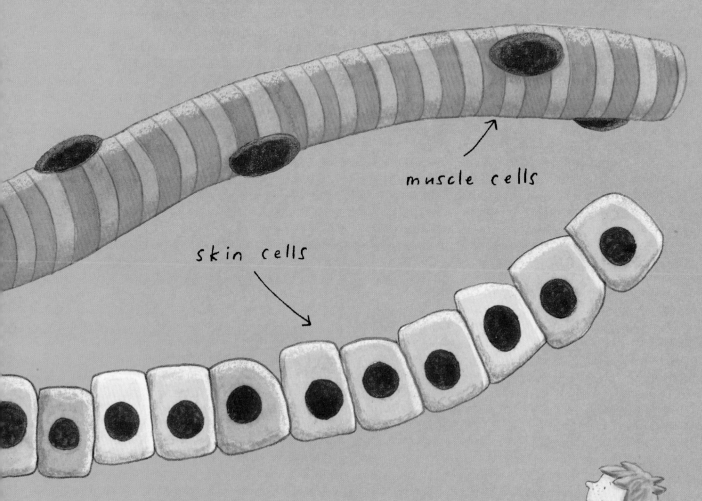

muscle cells

skin cells

Some of your **muscle cells** look
like long stripy strings, for example.
And some kinds of **skin cells**
are shaped like little cubes.
And there are **bone cells** that
look just like spiky blobs."

"Weird!" said Sam.
"But how do you know
they look like that?
Can you see them?"

microscope

"Not easily," said Mom.
"They're too small
to look at with just
your eyes. You'd need
a microscope to see
them at all."

Mom grinned. "There is a kind of **cell** that
you can see, though—
the yolk of a bird's egg.
In fact, the yolk of
an ostrich's egg
is the biggest
kind of **cell** in
the world!"

Mom picked up Sam's old sweater.

"Your **cells** are a little like the stitches in this sweater," she said. "Each one is very small, but when they join together they make something much bigger."

"Like building bricks," Sam said.

"That's right," said Mom. "Only your **cells** are all much much smaller than bricks or stitches."

"Yeah," said Sam. "So I must be made of millions and millions of **cells**."

"BILLIONS and BILLIONS," said Mom. "There are about 10,000,000,000 **cells** in just one of your thumbs!"

Sam peered at his thumb. "I still don't see how my body makes more **cells**, though. Where do they come from?"

"Well," said Mom, "what **cells** do is make
copies of themselves. It's very clever.
Each **cell** starts by growing
a little bigger.

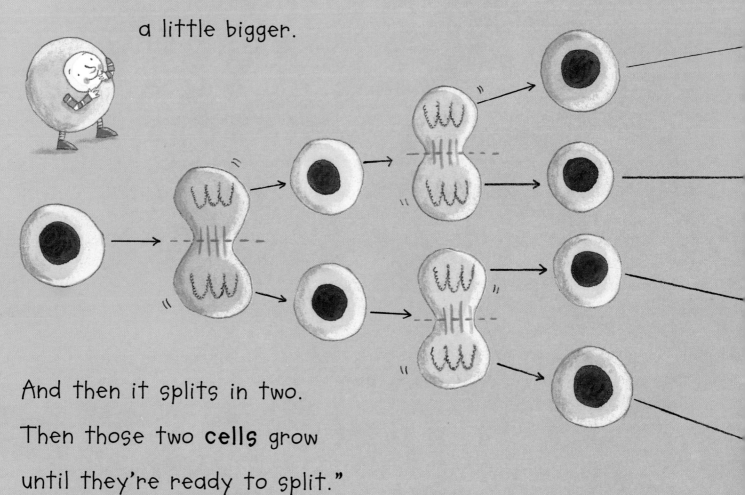

And then it splits in two.
Then those two **cells** grow
until they're ready to split."

"And they make four **cells**,"
Sam said. "Two times two is four."

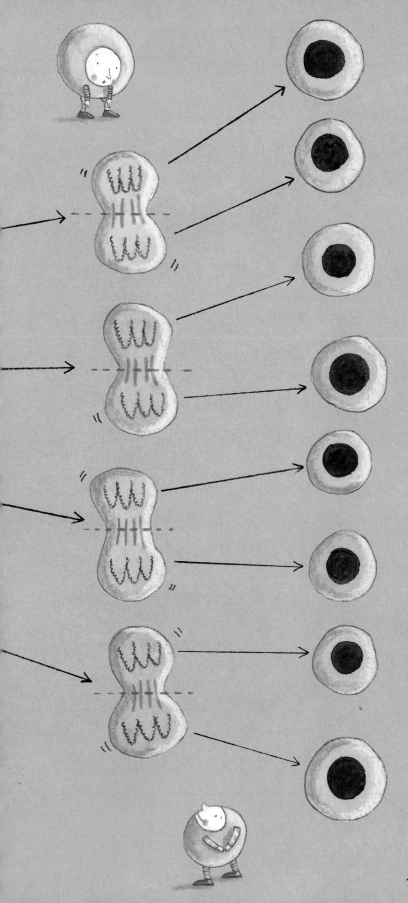

Mom smiled. "And what comes next? Two times four is?"

"Eight!" yelled Sam.

"Good," said Mom. "And two times eight is...?"

Sam grinned.
"A lot," he said.
"Do **cells** keep on making more and more **cells** forever and ever?"

23

"Some do," said Mom.
"Some kinds of **cells** are always wearing out and dying, so your body needs to make new ones to replace them.

You lose millions of **skin cells** every day, for example. They get rubbed off by your clothes or by washing, and lots just fall off by themselves."

24

"But not all your **cells** keep on making
more **cells** forever and ever," explained Mom,
"or you'd keep on growing forever and ever! When
you're about seventeen or eighteen years old,
for example, your **bone cells** will slow
right down and almost stop making
new **cells**. And that's when
you'll stop getting taller."

25

"Have all your **cells** slowed down?"
Sam asked.

Mom laughed.
"I'm certainly not
growing any taller!"

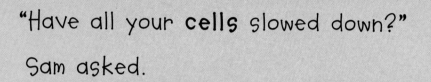

"I wish all my **cells**
would keep on growing,"
Sam said. "Then
I could be as tall as
a Tyrannosaurus rex!"

"Then you'd better hurry up
and help me put these things
away so we can have
breakfast," said Mom.
"**Cells** need feeding so
they can work properly!"

And she began to close the dresser drawers.

"MOM!" gasped Sam, and he giggled.

"You're busting out of your pants!"

Sam

cells